The
Little Book of
JOHN
DEERE

Foreword by Don Macmillan

A TOWN SQUARE BOOK
Voyageur Press

Edited by Michael Dregni
Designed by Andrea Rud
Printed in Hong Kong

04 05 5 4 3

Library of Congress Cataloging-in-Publication Data
The little book of John Deere / foreword by Don Macmillan.

    p. cm.
    Includes bibliographical references.
    ISBN 0-89658-577-8 (alk. paper)
    1. John Deere tractors—History.

TL233.6.J64 L58 2001
631.3'72'09—dc21

                    2001039020

Published by Voyageur Press, Inc.
123 North Second Street, P.O. Box 338,
Stillwater, MN 55082 U.S.A.
651-430-2210, fax 651-430-2211
books@voyageurpress.com
www.voyageurpress.com

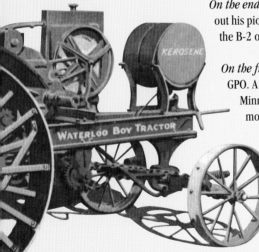

On the endsheets: Deere engineer Max Sklovsky tries out his pioneering all-wheel-drive tractor prototype, the B-2 of 1915–1916.

On the frontispiece: The nameplate of a Model GPO. A youngster tests the latest Deere at the Minnesota State Fair in the 1950s. Deere's modern 8300T crawler.

On the title pages, main photo: A farmwife calls the family to supper in Walter Haskell Hinton's famous painting. *Inset:* Deere poster advertising plows, sulky plows, and cultivators.

On the contents pages: John Deere's history told in a painting by Walter Haskell Hinton.

Contents

Foreword

Cultural Icon: The John Deere Legacy

By Don Macmillan

Don Macmillan is the world's most respected and best-known John Deere historian. He first drove a Deere Model AR in 1940. In 1958, he became Great Britain's first Deere dealer. In 1987, Deere appointed him to write *John Deere Tractors and Equipment,* Volumes 1 and 2. He is also the author of Voyageur Press's *The Big Book of John Deere Tractors*.

Some 197 years after John Deere's birth in 1804, the company that bears the blacksmith's name has risen to become the first and foremost farm-machinery maker in the world.

As a builder of tractors and ag equipment in North and South America, Europe, China, and India, Deere's title as Number One is justified. With the exception of Caterpillar, whose chief interest lies in other fields, Deere & Company is the sole farm-machinery maker to survive from its founding without being merged into or absorbed by other firms.

The company's road was long and hard from John Deere's blacksmith shop to becoming the world's largest maker of farm equipment. Deere committed itself fully to the newfangled farm tractor in 1918 with the purchase of the Waterloo Gasoline Engine Company and its renowned Waterloo Boy. Perhaps Deere's most famous tractor, the die-hard Model D, was introduced in 1923; production did not end until 1953, marking it as the longest-produced tractor ever.

It was not until 1956 that Deere truly became a global corporation, even though it had earlier exported machines to countries as far flung as England, Argen-

Dream Machines
Previous page: Like grandfather, like grandson. Allen Martin sits on his 1935 John Deere Model B while his grandson, Jonathan Martin, pilots a Model 60 pedal tractor. (Photograph by Keith Baum)

tina, and Russia. In 1956, Deere purchased Lanz of Germany, and the future course of Deere as a worldwide manufacturer was set.

Today's markets demand new and constantly developing technology and manufacturing techniques. With the introduction of its latest models, exciting prospects lie ahead for the Big Green line.

Yet whatever the future holds, the glories of Deere's past will always remain. Along the way to becoming the world's foremost tractor builder, Deere has produced the green machines that have found a place in the hearts of farmers and tractor lovers the world over. Deere's two-cylinder "Johnny Poppers" are for many the greatest tractors ever built. John Deere tractors have become a cultural icon of the farm.

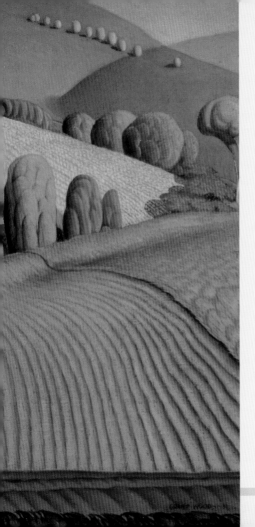

1

Heritage: The House That Plows Built

1804: John Deere is born in Rutland, Vermont, on February 7

1837: In Grand Detour, Illinois, blacksmith John Deere demonstrates his self-scouring steel plow fashioned from a saw blade

1848: John Deere moves production of his plow from Grand Detour to Moline, Illinois

1868: Deere & Co. incorporates with John Deere as president and his son, Charles Deere, as vice president

1886: John Deere dies at the age of eighty-two on May 17

I cut the teeth off with a hand chisel, with the help of a strike and sledge, then laid them on the fire of the forge and heated what little I could at a time and shaped them as best I could with the hand hammer . . . and finally succeeded in constructing a very rough plow.
—John Deere on the building of his first plow

Fall Plowing
Previous page: Iowa artist Grant Wood's 1931 oil painting celebrated the glory of farming. (Deere & Company)

John Deere's First Plow
Right: John Deere demonstrates in 1837 his self-scouring plow in this oil painting by Walter Haskell Hinton entitled *His Successful Moment.* Fashioned from a steel saw blade, Deere's polished plow broke the sticky prairie soil without gumming up.

The farmer of today proudly teaches his son what his own father taught him— to use a John Deere Plow.

Deere Plow Advertisement: "His First Lesson"

John Deere's Blacksmithery

Deere's re-created shop in Grand Detour, Illinois, features the tools and equipment the blacksmith used to craft his first plow in 1837. (Photograph by Ralph W. Sanders)

2
First Steps into the Tractor Field

1892: John Froelich of Iowa builds the world's first practical gas-powered tractor

1893: Froelich and others organize the Waterloo Gasoline Traction Engine Co. in Waterloo, Iowa

1912: Deere & Co. starts developing a gas tractor plow, the first of several experimental designs

1918: Debut of Henry Ford's revolutionary lightweight Fordson tractor

1918: Deere buys the Waterloo Gasoline Engine Co. and rights to the Waterloo Boy tractor

1918–1919: Deere's All-Wheel-Drive tractor engineered by Joseph Dain Sr. begins and ends production

1916 Waterloo Boy Model R

Previous page: Built by the Waterloo Gasoline Engine Co., the Waterloo Boy was a landmark lightweight gas tractor. Owner: Kent Kaster. (Photograph by Ralph W. Sanders)

Iowa Engineer and Custom Thresherman John Froelich

JOHN FROELICH.

Froelich Gas Tractor At Work

This famous photo is the sole image of a Froelich tractor during its brief heyday. In 1892, John Froelich mounted a 20-hp Van Duzen gas stationary engine on a wood frame with components from a Robinson & Co. steam traction engine. The Froelich was the first gas traction engine capable of powering itself forwards and backwards.

Deere All-Wheel-Drive Dain Tractor

In May 1914, Deere's Joseph Dain Sr. began building a gas tractor prototype. Just 100 examples of Dain's All-Wheel-Drive were built in 1918–1919 before Deere chose to produce the Waterloo Boy instead.

1917–1924 Waterloo Boy Model N

Waterloo Gasoline Engine Co. introduced its great Waterloo Boy in 1914. Powered by an overhead-valve, two-cylinder of 465 ci (7,617 cc), it made 25 belt hp. Deere built the N until 1924. Owner: Doug Peltzer. (Photograph by Hans Halberstadt)

1918 Deere Waterloo Boy Advertisement

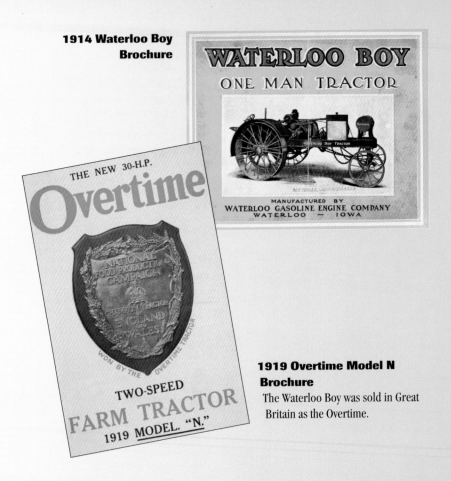

1914 Waterloo Boy Brochure

WATERLOO BOY
ONE MAN TRACTOR

MANUFACTURED BY
WATERLOO GASOLINE ENGINE COMPANY
WATERLOO — IOWA

THE NEW 30-H.P.
Overtime

NATIONAL
FOOD PRODUCTION
CAMPAIGN

CHAMPION TRACTOR
of
ENGLAND
and
WALES

WON BY THE OVERTIME TRACTOR

TWO-SPEED
FARM TRACTOR
1919 MODEL. "N."

1919 Overtime Model N Brochure

The Waterloo Boy was sold in Great Britain as the Overtime.

1930s Vindex 1/16-Scale Deere Combine
To offer a full line, Deere also began building combines and other farm equipment.
Owner: Ray Lacktorin.

3

Johnny Popper Replaces Old Dobbin

1923: Deere launches its Model D, an updated version of the Waterloo Boy and grandfather of all Deere tractors

1924: International Harvester debuts its general-purpose row-crop Farmall

1927: Deere introduces its own row-crop tractor, the C, which became the GP in 1928

1934–1935: Deere unveils its A and B, which become Deere's all-time best-selling tractors

1935–1938: The large G and small L fill out the Deere tractor line

1937: Deere celebrates its centennial

1930s Deere Model AO
Previous page: Deere's two-cylinder tractors were affectionately known as "Johnny Poppers" or "Poppin' Johnnies" due to the distinctive engine sound. Owner: Irv Baker. (Photographs by Hans Halberstadt)

1920s Deere Model D
Left: The D began as an update of the Waterloo Boy but was sold bearing the Deere name. This D has the 24-inch spoked flywheel on its side-by-side horizontal two-cylinder of 465 ci (7,617 cc) and 15 drawbar hp. (Photograph by Hans Halberstadt)

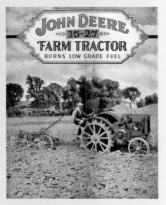

1927 Deere Model D Brochure

Olden Days and Modern Times

A grandfather tells his grandson of the advances in farming brought on by Deere's D in this painting by Walter Haskell Hinton.

1935–1938 Deere Model D

Introduced in 1923, the D remained in production for thirty years. (Photograph by Hans Halberstadt)

Starting the Deere Model D

Above: Farming was hard work in many ways: A farmer uses all his strength to turn his D's flywheel and start the engine. (Library of Congress)

1931 Deere Model GP

Facing page: Following the Farmall's success, Deere offered its own row-crop tractor, the C of 1926–1927. It was followed by the GP, introduced in 1928. The two-plow GP made 18.86 drawbar hp. A tricycle row-crop version of the GP, the GPWT, was built from 1929 to 1933. Owner: Tom Manning. (Photograph by Ralph W. Sanders)

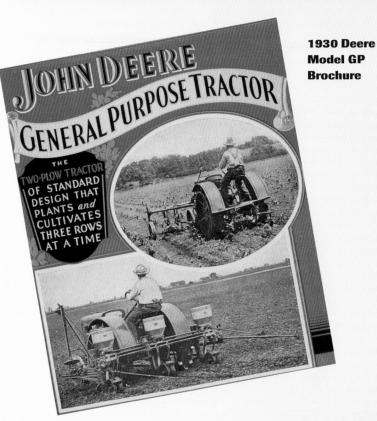

Everyone Wanted a Deere
Farming with a Deere gave Pa extra time to help Junior maintain
his soapbox tractor in this Walter Haskell Hinton painting.

*Probably no single stage in
the entire history of the company's
product development was any more
important than this one [the launch
of the Models A and B].*
—Wayne G. Broehl Jr.,
John Deere's Company

1936 Deere Model A

Deere's A replaced the GP in 1934 and
became one of the company's best-sellers
during its 1934–1952 production. Its 309-
ci (5,061-cc) two-cylinder put out 18.72
drawbar hp. An optional hydraulic lift
raised and lowered implements. Owner:
Tom Manning. (Photograph by Ralph W.
Sanders)

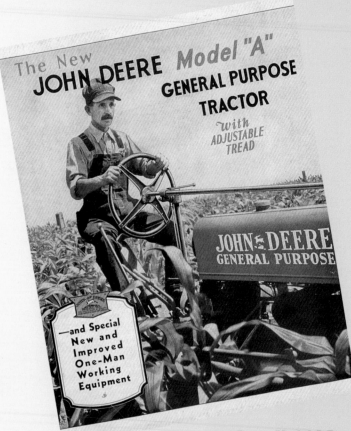

1933 Deere Model A Brochure

Ertl Precision Series 1/16-Scale Deere Model A

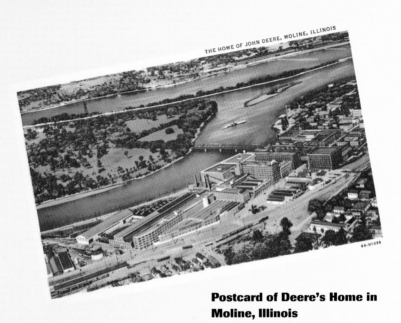

THE HOME OF JOHN DEERE, MOLINE, ILLINOIS

6A-H1035

**Postcard of Deere's Home in
Moline, Illinois**

1935 Deere Model AR
The standard-tread AR joined the line in 1935. The A was available in many variations,
including the AR, AO, AOS streamlined, AN, AW, ANH, AWH, and AI. Owner: Kent Kaster.
(Photograph by Ralph W. Sanders)

John Deere's early two-cylinder tractors were known variously as "Poppin' Johnnies" or "Johnny Poppers" as the engine's sound was so distinctive that farm wives could tell from the note of the engine when their husbands had idled down the tractor to come in for supper.
—*This Old Farm*

1941–1948 Deere Model AO
The A Orchard version featured large fenders, a low exhaust, and protective cowling so it did not damage trees as it worked. (Photograph by Hans Halberstadt)

1930s Deere Model BW

Introduced in 1935, the famous B featured a two-cylinder, 149-ci (2,441-cc) engine. The "W" suffix denoted a wide front end. Standard-tread BR, single-front-wheel BN, industrial BI, orchard BO wheeled and crawler versions, and Hi-Crop BNH and BWH models were all offered. (Photographs by Hans Halberstadt)

**1938 Deere Models
A and B Brochure**

1937 Deere Model BI

This BI wears the brilliant yellow paint
of Deere's Industrial models. The BI was
adapted from the standard-tread BR.
Owner: Kent Kaster. (Photograph by Ralph
W. Sanders)

A Seat When Day is Done

Right: A Deere tractor provides a place to rest when the work is over. (Library of Congress)

1940s Deere Model BO

Facing page: The orchard BO was dressed up with full fenders, a wide front, cowling over hood-top fixtures, and a low exhaust pipe so the tractor did not damage trees. Owner: Doug Peltzer. (Photograph by Hans Halberstadt)

*I have not heard many farmers rhapsodize
about machines, except perhaps for ones they used
during childhood—two-cylinder Deere tractors
or one of the early Farmalls.*
—Verlyn Klinkenborg, *Making Hay*

1940s Deere Model BO-L

Lindeman Manufacturing of Yakima, Washington,
converted Deere models to crawlers, including this
orchard BO. Deere bought Lindeman in 1947. (Photograph by Hans Halberstadt)

4

Heinrich Lanz: The German Connection

1838: Heinrich Lanz born in Germany

1859: Heinrich Lanz's factory established in Mannheim, Germany, building steam engines and threshers

1902: Lanz meets Charles Deere, inspiring him and his son, Karl Lanz, to expand production and mechanization

1911: Lanz starts buildings its first tractor, the Landbaumotor

1921: Dr. Fritz Huber designs the semi-diesel hot-bulb Bulldog, Lanz's most famous tractor

1956: Deere purchases Lanz and continues tractor production in Mannheim for its worldwide markets

1954 Lanz B Bulldog D2806

Previous page: Lanz became famous the world over for its Bulldog model engineered by Dr. Fritz Huber and launched in 1921. The Bulldog was the world's first hot-bulb-fired, crude-oil-burning tractor. Owner: Daniel Binet. (Photograph by Andrew Morland)

1920s Lanz HR2 D2088 Bulldog Brochure

1939 Lanz HR9 Eil Bulldog

Introduced in 1937, Lanz's "Speedy" Bulldog boasted a comfortable driving environment protected by a full windshield; open- and closed-cab versions were available. With 55 hp from a 629-ci (10,303-cc) engine, these Bulldog road models had five or six forward gears and a top speed of 25 mph (40 km/h). Owner: Pierre Bouillé. (Photograph by Andrew Morland)

1930s Lanz Bulldog Brochure

**1960s Deere–Lanz 300 and 500
Brochure**

1960s Deere–Lanz 300
After Deere bought Lanz in 1956, tractor production continued at Mannheim with the former Lanz works building Deere tractors for the worldwide market. (Photograph by Chester Peterson Jr.)

5
Styling Comes to the Farmyard

1938: Industrial designer Henry Dreyfuss gives the Deere A and B a styling facelift; the rest of Deere's line is soon also streamlined

1939: Deere launches its small, one-plow H, designed to replace the last horse team on the farm

1939: Ford unveils its revolutionary Ford-Ferguson Model 9N with hydraulics and three-point equipment mounting

1947: Deere buys crawler specialist Lindeman Manufacturing of Yakima, Washington

1959: Deere offers its 200-hp, four-wheel-drive 8010, heralding the demise of the two-cylinder Deere tractor

Just Like Pa

Previous page: While Pa eats his lunch, Junior and Spot pretend they are piloting the family's "Poppin' Johnny" in this painting by Walter Haskell Hinton.

1941 Deere Model H Brochure

1940s Deere Model HWH

Styling came to Deere's green machines via industrial designer Henry Dreyfuss, who gave the "unstyled" A and B a modern facelift in 1938. The H debuted in 1939 with styled bodywork. This Hi-Crop, wide-front tractor was a rarity built only in 1941–1942. Owner: Doug Peltzer. (Photograph by Hans Halberstadt)

Pint-Sized Shadow

Above: Junior slathered his toy Deere in oil while Pa greased the Roll-O-Matic front end of his styled A in this 1949 painting.

1948 Deere Model M

Facing page: Deere debuted its utility M after World War II powered by a new vertical two-cylinder engine of 18 drawbar hp. Advanced Touch-O-Matic hydraulics made implement control convenient. The M was built in a new factory in Dubuque, Iowa. Owner: Ron Jungmeyer. (Photograph by Ralph W. Sanders)

"Tom Brent and his Tractor"

Many a 4-H youth learned how to maintain the family's tractor from this famous book. Naturally, a Deere graced the cover.

**1940s Arcade
1/16-Scale Deere
Model A**

**1938 Deere Models A
and B Styled Brochure**

A Friend In Need
Facing page: With Sis
tagging along, Junior
brings his toy Deere into
the local dealership for
repairs in this Walter
Haskell Hinton painting.

GREATER **VALUE**

they're TOMORROW

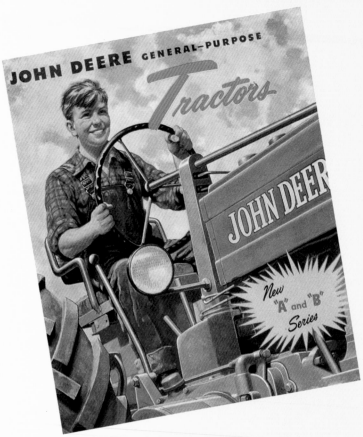

1947 Deere Models A and B Styled Brochure

Ertl 1/16-Scale Deere Late Model A

How could anyone at all interested in the history, culture, mechanics of agriculture ignore the remarkable role of John Deere green? The John Deere has become almost a transcendent, universal icon for the phrase "old tractor."

—Roger Welsch

1940s Deere Model LA

At the small-tractor end of Deere's line, the LA offered more power than its L predecessor. The roots of the model stretch back to the 1936 Y and 1937 62. The LA was built from 1940 to 1946. (Photograph by Hans Halberstadt)

**1941 Deere
Models L and LA
Brochure**

Going Places

Everyone wanted to hitch a ride on a Deere
because a farmer with a Deere was
certainly going places.

Tractors changed everything. Never mind the rest of the world counted time as B.C. or A.D., for agriculture the ages were either B.T. or A.T., Before Tractor or After. Never mind no one else understood, the farmer did.
—Justin Isherwood, "Tractors,"
Book of Plough

1940s Deere Model R

Deere's first diesel tractor, the R, was unveiled in 1948. Started by a two-cylinder gas "pony" engine, the 416-ci (6,817-cc) two-cylinder diesel created 51 PTO hp. (Photograph by Hans Halberstadt)

*We love old tractors because old
tractors have souls.*
—Roger Welsch,
100 Years of Vintage Farm Tractors

1953 Deere Model 40
Deere updated its old Letter Series to the
Number Series tractors starting in 1952.
Based on the earlier MT, the small 40 was
introduced in 1953. Its vertical two-
cylinder engine was common to the other
Deeres made at the Dubuque facility.
Owner: Mark Hild. (Photograph by Ralph
W. Sanders)

1954 Deere Model 70 Diesel Brochure

BRAND SPANKIN' NEW

THE JOHN DEERE "70" DIESEL

1953 Deere Model 70
Deere's large G was replaced by the 70 in 1953, when liquified petroleum gas, or LPG, also became a fuel option on the 70 and 60. Owners: Bob and Mark Hild. (Photograph by Ralph W. Sanders)

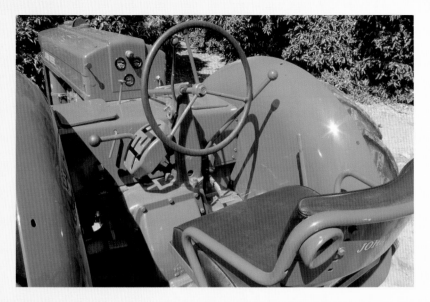

1950s Deere Model 60
Above: Cockpit comforts were far advanced in the new Number Series from the first Deere tractors. (Photograph by Hans Halberstadt)

1955 Deere Model 50
Facing page: Deere's venerable B tractor was replaced in 1952 with the 50. This 1953 row-crop tricycle had the new Duplex Carburetion, live power takeoff (PTO), high pressure Powr-Trol hydraulics, and rack-and-pinion rear wheel width adjustment. Owner: Bob Hild. (Photograph by Ralph W. Sanders)

1959 Deere Model 830

The 20 Series replaced the Numbered Series and was in turn replaced by the 30 Series. The big 830 was Deere flagship model in 1959–1960, boasting 69 drawbar and 75 belt hp. The 830 represented the ultimate in Deere two-cylinder development. (Photograph by Chester Peterson Jr.)

Lyle Dingman 1/16-Scale Deere Model 830

1956 Deere 20 Series Brochure

Restoration II

Restoring old iron has become a hobby of
farmers everywhere. Iowa artist Charles
Freitag captured the appeal of tractor
restoration in his painting of a grandfather
at work on his 730 while his grandsons
help out and work on their Deere pedal
tractor. (Apple Creek Publishing)

6

A New Generation of Power

1960: D-Day, August 29: Deere launches its New Generation of Power tractors powered by tradition-breaking four- and six-cylinder engines

1968: Deere contracts Wagner Tractor Co. of Portland, Oregon, to build the WA-14 and WA-17 articulated four-wheel drives, foreshadowing the shape of tractors to come

1972: Deere Generation II tractors are unveiled on August 19 with innovative Sound-Gard bodies featuring revolutionary safety and comfort

1973: Deere celebrates fifty years of building tractors

1960s Deere 4000 Diesel

Previous page: The beloved two-cylinder line ended in 1960 when Deere's New Generation of Power was announced. Some dealers and farmers were sad, others were glad. (Photograph by Chester Peterson Jr.)

1960 Deere 3010 and 4010 Brochure

1959 Deere 8010

The first sign of the momentous changes in Deere's future was the 1959 debut of the 215-hp articulated 8010 tractor and its integral eight-bottom plow. The 8010 signalled the end of the two-cylinder era in the United States and the single-cylinder era in Europe. Owners: Walter and Bruce Keller. (Photograph by Chester Peterson Jr.)

Ertl 1/16-Scale Deere 3010

1960s Deere 4020 Hi-Crop

Introduced in 1960, Deere's 4020 was one of the most significant tractors in farming history—and thus became one of the most copied. At the heart of the 4020 was its revolutionary hydraulic system that supplied pressure for raising implements and ran the power steering, power brakes, and differential lock. (Photograph by Chester Peterson Jr.)

1960s Deere 3020 Orchard

Deere's fully enclosed Orchard tractors appeared like streamlined race cars.

1960s Deere 5020 Hot Rod

This 5020 was converted to V-8 power with a Detroit Diesel 8V71 engine. Owner: Jon Kinzenbaw. (Photograph by Chester Peterson Jr.)

1960s Deere WA-14 and WA-17 Brochure

Deere contracted with the Wagner Tractor Co. of Portland, Oregon, to build the 225-hp WA-14 and 280-hp turbo WA-17. The Wagners filled the slot until Deere had its 7020 and 7520 ready for the market in 1970.

1970s Deere 4320

Debuting in 1970, the 4320 was a turbocharged "super" 4020 boasting 115 hp. (Photograph by Chester Peterson Jr.)

**Ertl 1/16-Scale
Deere 7020**

1965 Deere 8020

Deere updated its 8010 as the 8020 in 1965, but the massive articulated tractor was still ahead of its time. Owner: Jeff McManus. (Photograph by Chester Peterson Jr.)

7
Global John Deere

1987: Deere celebrates its 150th anniversary

1997: Deere launches its flagship crawler 8000T Series, followed by the 9000T of 1999

1998: Deere marks eighty years of building tractors

Present: Deere builds tractors for the world market with factories in North America, South America, South Africa, Europe, India, China, Turkey, and elsewhere around the globe

1982 Deere 8850

Previous page: When launched in 1982, the 8850 was the most powerful Deere ever—and foretold the shape of Deere's future with larger and more powerful machines.

1978 Deere 8440 and 8640 Brochure

1993 Deere 70 Series Brochure

1998 Deere 6410

The 6000 Series introduced in 1998 heralded Deere's new marketing philosophy of building a "world tractor." The 6000 Series was built in Mannheim while the 7000 siblings were constructed in Waterloo. Both were sold around the globe.

**Ertl 1/16-Scale
Deere 9400**

1994 Deere 8300

Deere's 8000 Series tractors were the company's largest two-wheel-drive machines ever. With 200 hp on tap, the 8300 was an awesome farm machine.

1999 Deere 9300T
With the launch of the
8000T rubber-track series
in 1997, Deere offered
crawler and wheeled
version of its flagship line.
The 9000T Series of 1999
upped the ante with an
even larger tractor capable
of the heaviest-duty jobs on
the farm.

Bibliography

Baldwin, Nick, and Andrew Morland. *Classic Tractors of the World*. Stillwater, Minnesota: Voyageur Press, 1998.

Macmillan, Don. *The Big Book of John Deere Tractors*. Stillwater, Minnesota: Voyageur Press, 1999.

Pripps, Robert N., and Andrew Morland. *The Big Book of Farm Tractors*. Stillwater, Minnesota: Voyageur Press, 2001.

Pripps, Robert N., and Andrew Morland. *The Field Guide to Vintage Farm Tractors*. Stillwater, Minnesota: Voyageur Press, 1999.

Sanders, Ralph W. *Ultimate John Deere*. Stillwater, Minnesota: Voyageur Press, 2001.

Sanders, Ralph W. *Vintage Farm Tractors*. Stillwater, Minnesota: Voyageur Press, 1996.

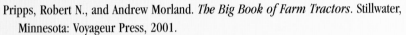

All in the Family
Facing page: Faith in Deere farm tractors often runs in the family and is passed down from generation to generation. Brian H. Thompson stands with his Deere 4620 behind a future generation of Deere fans. (Photograph by Chester Peterson Jr.)

Deere's 1880 Trademark

Deere's 1885 trademark

Deere's 1912 Trademark

Waterloo Boy's 1913 Logo

Lanz's 1930 Trademark

Deere's 1936 Trademark

Deere's 2000 Trademark

Deere's 1968 Trademark